W9-BCQ-508

Dutch & delicious

Typically Dutch food
and beverages

FOOD, FUN & FACTS FROM HOLLAND

Dutch & delicious

Typically Dutch food
and beverages

Credits

Photo editing and design: Verba bv, Ede
Photo's: Shutterstock.com; TypicalMedia.com; M. van Zwieten; Flip de Ruiter; Irene Verbeek
We advise you to contact the local tourist office before you decide to visit a tourist attraction.
The tourist office has the latest information on opening hours and prices.
The editor and publisher are in no way responsible for the consequences of any changes in the information in this publication.

All rights reserved. No part of this publication may be reproduced, stored in a retrieval system, or transmitted by any means, mechanical, photocopying, recording or otherwise, without the prior permission of the copyright holder.

www.lantaarnpublishers.nl

© Verba bv
© Copyright for this edition: De Lantaarn bv, Ede
NUR 442
ISBN 978-94-6188-727-6

Contents

Keukenhof, Lisse, Zuid-Holland

6

Dutch Nostalgia

When people are asked what is typically Dutch, they will usually talk about the lakes, rivers and canals and the fact that the country is extremely flat. For a large part of the Netherlands this is very true, but there is more to this small country than water, polders and the flat countryside in the North: just think about the hills in the southern province of Limburg, the forests in the Achterhoek and Drenthe, and the historical cities in the West, near the coast. The diversity in landscapes is reflected in the Dutch cuisine. The Dutch cuisine has always been strongly influenced by other cultures and traditions, and the Dutch are extremely interested in foreign foods and cooking.

This book however will focus on traditional Dutch recipes: rather straight-forward dishes without any fuss.

Read and discover, cook and try!

Dijkkerk in Dodewaard, Gelderland

Jordaan, Amsterdam

Neeltje Jans, Zeeland

MENU'S

Frites met:

Frikandel

Gehaktbal

Schnitzel

Kip-saté

Kibbeling

Amsterdam

Zaanse Schans, Noord

8

A Closer Look at the Netherlands

The Netherlands are divided into twelve provinces. Of course there are many similarities in terms of landscape, but the differences between provinces that are further apart are quite substantial – especially when one compares the province of Limburg with its hills to for example Flevoland with its empty polders of reclaimed land.

Almost twenty percent of the Netherlands consists of water, and a large part of the country is actually below sea level. The people are protected by dykes, dams, sluices, levees, locks, and storm surge barriers. Water management and in particular the Delta Works in the southwestern province of Zeeland is one of the things this country is renowned for.

The Netherlands have a rich history both in landscape and in urban development. Traces from very long ago are for example the many dolmens in Drenthe, the huge whale jawbones on the island of Schiermonnikoog and the many characteristic buildings in the Dutch cities.

The oldest cities – Nijmegen and Voorburg – date back to the time of the Roman Empire. Later, many more cities were founded, of which the cities that were part of the Hanseatic League are considered to be very attractive. The three largest cities of the Netherlands are Amsterdam, Rotterdam with its port, and The Hague where the government resides.

Blaak, Rotterdam

Rotterdam

Cheese market in Gouda, Zuid-Holland

10

Ketelbrug, Flevoland

Cities in the Netherlands are popular because of their history, culture, shops and night life.
Also typically Dutch are the windmills of the Zaanse Schans and Kinderdijk, the traditional fishing villages of Urk, Volendam and Marken, the cheese markets in Gouda and Alkmaar, and the tulips in the Keukenhof in Lisse.
And if you want to see all of the Netherlands in just one day, you can go to Madurodam – a miniature park with Holland's highlights.

Madurodam, The Hague

Belt Schutsloot, Overijssel

Scheveningen near The Hague

12

The rivers, the long North Sea coast, the islands in the North and the lakes in especially Friesland are very popular with water sports enthusiasts. Miles and miles of cycle paths cover the entire country and even the largest woodland area, National Park Hoge Veluwe.

The fact that more than ten million tourists from abroad visit the Netherlands every year, surely says something about the popularity of this relatively small country with seventeen million inhabitants.

Veluwe, Gelderland

Zwolle, Overijssel

Typically Dutch

Each part of the Netherlands has its own culture and traditions, but some traditions are nation-wide. They can be so very common that the Dutch themselves don't realize how Dutch they really are.

For example, there is the Dutch *bakkie*, 'cuppa' – which is almost always a cup of coffee, enjoyed in the company of neighbours, family or friends. With their *bakkie* coffee the Dutch have a small cookie or a slice of cake. Quite often this cake will be gingerbread, usually with a dollop of real butter.

In cold winters, the Dutch venture onto the ice to go skating – the Dutch are so good at it that they have dominated the skating events at the Olympics and other international tournaments for decades. A century ago people used bones and pieces of wood to make skates, later they invented skates with fixed shoes and in the 1980s a Dutchman – who else? – invented the hinging 'clap' skate, which broke numerous records.

Due to climate change, the winters are less cold now and there is more rain, which is something the Dutch love to complain about.

Zaanse Schans, Noord-Holland

Schiermonnikoog, an island in the North

Kinderdijk, Zuid-Holland

To warm the spirits and body, Dutch grownups may drink a *kopstoot* (head-butt), referring to a small glass of gin (*jenever*) downed in one go, followed by a glass of beer.

When it does or doesn't rain in the Netherlands, it is usually very windy, and that is the reason why there are so many wind turbines along the coast and in the flat countryside. The development of the modern wind turbines started long ago with the traditional wind mill, of which there are still about 1170 left.

The Netherlands are also famous for the flower bulbs and colourful tulip fields. Another classic are the wooden shoes or clogs (*klompen*), although nowadays you won't see that many Dutchmen wearing them.

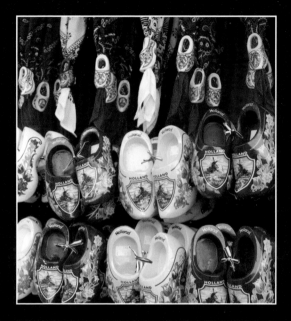

Amsterdam

Almost every Dutch citizen owns at least one bike, and the Netherlands boasts thousands of kilometres of cycle paths.

Cheese is the most popular sandwich filling: on average, the Dutch eat over 15 kilos a year! In the sixteenth century, the rich would eat this sandwich from a plate of Delft Blue, but nowadays this kind of tableware is mainly collected and not used. Before, folkloric costumes were worn in some towns, with variations in appearance per town, but nowadays, regional attire is mainly worn on holidays, if at all.

A widespread Dutch holiday is *Sinterklaas* (the original Santa Clause) on December 5, when children (and many adults as well) get presents, although some grownups are even more dedicated to this holiday than the kids.

Arrival of Sinterklaas

Keukenhof, Lisse, Zuid-Holland

Dutch Regional Dishes

Each province of the Netherlands has its very own character, traditions, dishes and delights. Some of these regional dishes were forgotten – even in the Netherlands – and can only be found in old cookbooks or notebooks with recipes written by cooks and maids. Although these recipes tend to be very regional, they are sometimes found in various parts of the country, probably because cooks and maids would take them with them when they moved. A recipe like Jan-in-de-zak ('John in the bag'), for example, can be found all over the country, though under different names. Another striking aspect is that although sometimes the dishes are the same, ingredients and preparation may vary per province, region or even town.

In this book, we present you with a selection of Dutch dishes and delights, such as Mussel Soup, Speculaas and Grandma's Apple Tart.

Never tried these?
Never even heard of them?
Go on and try the following recipes!

Begijnhof, Amsterdam

Brown Bean Soup

Ingredients
400 g canned brown beans
1 fresh sausage
¾ litre water
1 onion
1 leek

Preparation
Chop the onion. Clean the leek and cut into rings.
Add beans, sausage, water, onion and leek to a large saucepan and cook for almost 1 hour over a medium heat.
Remove the sausage from the pan and cut into slices. Add to the pan again. Season with salt, pepper, and if you like a bit of sambal (chilli paste).

Mussel Soup

Preparation

Wash and rinse the mussels in salted cold water.
Finely chop the onion. Add onion, parsley and celery leaves
to a medium saucepan. Place the mussels on top.
Add about 250 ml fresh water. Cook 10 minutes until the
mussels have opened; shake the pan once or twice.
Save 8 mussels in their shells. Take the remaining mussels
from their shell and sieve the cooking liquid. Add water
to make 1 litre.
Cut the celeriac and carrots into cubes and the leek into
rings. Heat the butter in a large saucepan and sauté the
celeriac, carrots and leek. Add the cooking liquid, stock cube
and lentils and cook for 20 minutes.
Throw away any mussels that are still closed. Add the
mussels to the pan, season with finely chopped parsley,
salt and pepper. Garnish the soup with the mussels in their
shell.

Ingredients

serves 4:
1 kg fresh mussels
1 onion
celery leaves
parsley
½ celeriac
200 g carrots
1 leek
25 g butter
1 stock cube
600 g lentils, cooked
salt and pepper

Frisian Onion Soup
'Sipelsop'

Ingredients
4 eggs
500 g onions
60 g butter
60 g plain flour
1 litre stock
salt
freshly ground pepper
nutmeg
1 tsp vinegar
100 g grated Frisian clove cheese
bread

Sipelsop is het Frisian word for onion soup, and this variation is at least as good as the French onion soup.

Preparation
Boil the eggs 8 minutes until hard.
Peel and chop the onions. Heat the butter in a frying pan and sauté the onion until transparent. Add the flour and whisk in the stock. Bring to the boil and cook for 5 minutes over a low heat. Season to taste with salt, pepper and nutmeg.
Stir in the vinegar. Peel the eggs. Take 4 deep plates, put an egg in each plate and chop finely. Divide the soup over the plates and serve with grated clove cheese.
Serve with slices of white bread.

Pea Soup
'Snert'

Preparation

Take a large saucepan and add the rinsed split peas, hock, bacon and 3 litres of water. Bring to the boil. Skim and leave to simmer for another 5 minutes. Remove the hock and bacon from the soup and cut into slices. Add the hock and bacon to the pan again.

Add the celeriac, carrot, onion, potato and the whole smoked sausage. Bring to the boil and leave to simmer for 30 minutes. Add the finely chopped leek, parsley and celery leaves and season to taste with salt, pepper and stock cubes. Stir to prevent the soup from burning.

Ingredients
for 7 litres:
500 g split peas
1 hock of pork, including bone
150 g streaky bacon
1 celeriac, cubed
1 large carrot, sliced
1 onion, finely chopped
1 big potato, cubed
1 smoked sausage
1 leek
½ bunch of parsley
½ bunch of leaves
salt and pepper
3 stock cubes

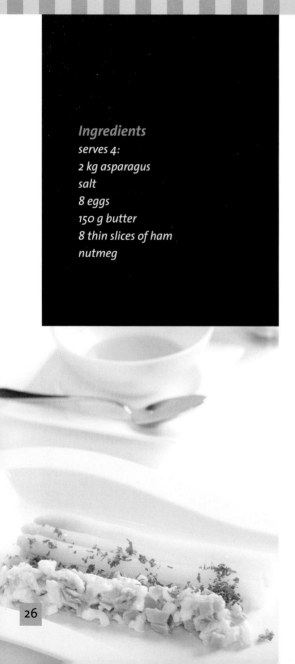

Asparagus

Preparation

Peel the asparagus with a peeler, starting from the top. Cut off the woody ends and tie the asparagus shoots together to a bundle.

Add plenty of water to a large saucepan. Add the asparagus shoots and a little salt and boil for 45 minutes until soft. Hard-boil the eggs. Melt the butter. Roll up the slices of ham. Place the cooked asparagus in a warm dish (you can used the cooking liquid to make soup) and serve the eggs, melted butter and ham separately.

Eating asparagus the Dutch way
Finely chop 2 hardboiled eggs, place on a plate and stir in the melted butter to make a creamy sauce. Chop up the ham and stir into the sauce. Season to taste with nutmeg. Pick up an asparagus with your hand. Dip in the egg sauce and take a bite.
Serve with baby potatoes.
Asparagus are best served on the day you buy them. Keep them no longer than a day in a cool place (not in the fridge), rolled up in a moist towel.

Ingredients
serves 4:
2 kg asparagus
salt
8 eggs
150 g butter
8 thin slices of ham
nutmeg

Mashed Potatoes and Kale
'Boerenkoolstamppot'

Preparation

Wash and finely chop the kale and cook for 10 minutes. Add the peeled and cubed potatoes to a large saucepan, sprinkle with sugar and cover with water. Place the sausage and kale on top.

Cover the pan, bring to the boil and leave to simmer for about 30 minutes. Drain and remove the sausage. Mash the potatoes and kale, stir in the butter and season to taste with pepper, salt and vinegar. Cut the sausage into slices and add to the *boerenkool*.

Ingredients

serves 4:
500 g fresh kale
1 kg potatoes
200 ml water
1 tsp sugar
1 fresh smoked sausage
15 g butter
1 tbsp vinegar
black pepper, freshly ground
salt

Mashed Potatoes and Beans
'Naked buttocks in a green field'

Ingredients
250 g white beans
1¼ litre water
1 kg potatoes
500 g string beans
1 smoked sausage
100 ml milk
25 g butter
salt
freshly ground pepper

Preparation
Wash and rinse the white beans and leave to soak for 24 hours. Bring the beans and the salted water to the boil and simmer for 1 hour until soft.
Peel and cut the potatoes into cubes.
Wash the string beans and cut them using a bean slicer.
Place the potatoes in a large saucepan and cover with water; add the sliced string beans and a little salt.
Bring to the boil and cook for 30 minutes until soft.
Place the sausage in hot but not boiling water for 15 minutes.
Drain the white beans in a colander. Drain the potatoes and string beans; mash with the lukewarm milk, butter, salt and pepper until smooth. Fold in the white beans.
Serve the 'naked buttocks in the green field' on a preheated serving plate and place the sausage on top.

Onion and Beef Hash

Preparation

Cut the beef into cubes, season with salt and pepper, and dust with flour. Mix well. Heat the butter and fat in a frying pan and brown the beef. Add the sliced onions, bay leaves, cloves, sugar and vinegar. Add water to cover the beef and put a lid on the pan. Stew for 3 hours; add a slice of bacon after 2½ hours.

Thicken the juices with a little corn flour, mixed with water. Serve the hash with mash(ed potatoes).

Ingredients
600 g beef chunk or rump
salt and pepper
plain flour
75 g butter
2 tbsp beef tallow
1 kg onions
2 bay leaves
3 cloves
2 tsp sugar
2 tbsp vinegar
bacon
corn flour

Mashed Potatoes with Apples
'Hot lightning'

Ingredients
250 ml water
½ tsp salt
5 peppercorns
1 bay leaf
½ tsp mace
400 g brisket
1½ kg potatoes
500 g cooking apples
1 kg firm apples
75 g butter

Preparation
Take a large saucepan and add water, salt, peppercorns, bay leaf and mace. Bring to the boil. Add the brisket and leave to simmer for 1½ hours.

In the meantime, peel the potatoes and cut into cubes.

Take 2 cooking apples, peel, remove core and slice the apples into 2 cm thick slices.

Peel and quarter the rest of the apples, and remove the core. Add the potatoes and quartered apples to the pan with the brisket and leave to simmer for another 30 minutes.

Remove the brisket from the pan and drain the potatoes and apples. Do not throw away the cooking liquid.

Mash the potatoes and apples with 50 g butter and add enough cooking liquid to make a smooth mash.

Heat the remaining butter in a frying pan and fry the apple slices until they are golden brown.

Transfer the mash to a preheated dish and place the fried apples and the sliced beef on top.

Mash with Carrots and Onions

Preparation

Take a large saucepan and add the brisket, 300 ml boiling water and a little salt. Leave to simmer for 1 hour.

Add the potatoes, carrots and onions. Bring to the boil and leave to simmer for about 30 minutes. Remove the beef from the pan and keep warm. Drain the cooking liquid and keep separate. Mash the potatoes, onions and carrots; mix well. Stir in the cooking liquid, the butter and if necessary the hot milk.

Cut the beef into slices and serve with the mash.

Ingredients

400 g brisket
boiling water
salt
1¼ kg carrots, cleaned and sliced
1½ kg potatoes, peeled
400 g onions, peeled and chopped
80-100 g butter
75 ml hot milk

Pancakes

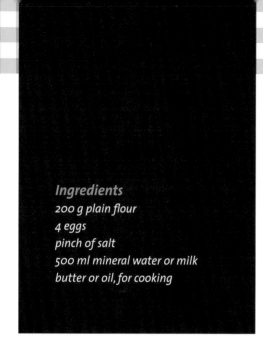

Ingredients
200 g plain flour
4 eggs
pinch of salt
500 ml mineral water or milk
butter or oil, for cooking

Preparation
Mix the flour, eggs and salt in a large bowl. Stir in the mineral water or milk and leave to rest at room temperature for about 30 minutes.
Heat the butter or oil in a large non-stick frying pan.
Add a ladle of batter to the pan and cook the pancake over a medium heat for about 2 minutes on each side. Repeat with the remaining batter. Serve the pancakes with syrup or icing sugar.

Variation: also try pancakes with slices of cheese, bacon or apple.

WATCH OUT!

Don't use Koopmans for this!

bon appetit

Mashed Potatoes and Endive

Preparation

Peel the potatoes and boil in salted water.
In the meantime, fry the bacon in a dry frying pan.
Remove the tough stems from the endive and cut up
the leaves. Wash and drain thoroughly.
Mash the cooked potatoes and stir in the butter and
hot milk. Rapidly stir in the raw endive and add the
crispy bacon and cheese. Season to taste with pepper
and serve immediately.

Ingredients
2 kg potatoes
15 g salt
150 g cubed bacon
750 g broad-leafed endive
100 g butter
300 ml milk, hot
100 g cheese, cubed
pepper

Mash Potatoes and Lettuce

Ingredients
1½ kg potatoes
250 g streaky bacon, cubed
600 g lettuce
500 ml milk
25 g butter
½ tsp salt
pinch of nutmeg

Preparation

Peel and rinse the potatoes and cut into cubes. Add the potatoes and about 250 ml of water to a large saucepan and cook for 20 minutes until soft.

In the meantime, fry the bacon over a low heat. Remove damaged leaves from the lettuce, wash the remaining lettuce, drain and chop. Bring the milk to the boil in a small saucepan. Drain the potatoes and mash with butter, salt, nutmeg and the hot milk. Next, stir in the lettuce and heat very briefly (you don't want the lettuce to cook).

Pile the mash onto a preheated serving plate and drizzle with the crispy bacon and fat from the frying pan.

Devil's Bread

Preparation

Melt the butter in a small pan over a low heat, turn off the heat and leave to cool.

Sieve the flour over a large bowl and add salt and cinnamon. Heat the milk until lukewarm and stir in the yeast until dissolved. Make a little well in the flour and pour in the yeasty milk and the melted butter. Gradually add the remaining lukewarm milk and knead into a nice and smooth dough. Keep kneading the dough for about 15 minutes. Cover with a moist tea towel and leave to rise for 1 hour in a warm place. Grease a baking tray with butter. Divide the dough into two parts and shape into pointy rolls. Place them on the baking tray, cover and leave to rise for 30 minutes.

Preheat the oven to 200 °C. Make two 5 cm cuts into each pointy end (for the devil's hooves) and fold the cuts back. Whisk the egg and spread onto the breads. Bake the breads for 35 minutes until golden brown and nicely done.

Ingredients
- 50 g butter
- 500 g plain flour
- pinch of salt
- 1½ tsp cinnamon
- 200 ml milk
- 30 g yeast
- 1 egg

Fried Eggs

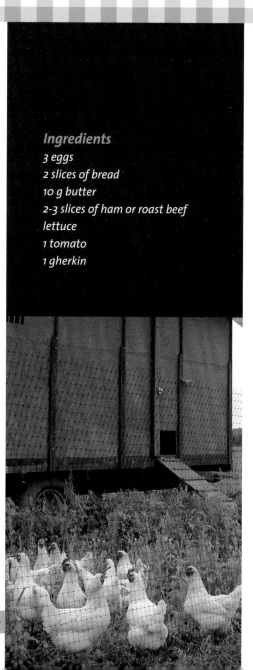

Ingredients
3 eggs
2 slices of bread
10 g butter
2-3 slices of ham or roast beef
lettuce
1 tomato
1 gherkin

Preparation
Place a couple of lettuce leaves onto a plate. Put the slices of bread on top, spread with butter and top with ham or roast beef. Cut the tomato and gherkin into slices.
Heat a little butter in a frying pan and fry the eggs.
Place onto the ham. Garnish with tomato and gherkin.
Season to taste with salt and pepper.

French Toast
'Twisting bitches'

Preparation

Whisk together the eggs and milk in a bowl. Stir in the cinnamon. Dip in a slice of bread and leave to soak for a bit. Take out the slice of bread and leave to drain.
In the meantime, melt the butter in a frying pan. Fry the soaked slice of bread on both sides. If you use a large frying pan, you can fry several slices at the same time. Sprinkle the French toast with sugar or serve with jam.

Variation: this toast is also very nice with fresh fruit or with sugar and cinnamon.

Ingredients
serves 4:
12 slices of stale white bread
5 eggs
300 ml milk
2 tsp cinnamon
butter
sugar or jam

Brandy and Raisins
'Farm boys'

Ingredients
100 ml water
10 cloves
1 cinnamon stick
100 g sugar
500 g raisins
1 litre brandy
2 preserving bottles of 750 ml

Preparation
In a small pan bring to the boil water, cloves and stick of cinnamon; leave to simmer for 10 minutes. Add sugar and stir to dissolve. Remove the pan from the heat and remove cloves and cinnamon from the pan.

Wash and rinse the raisins. Add to the pan and leave to soak for several hours in the spicy sugar water. When cooled, divide over the two clean bottles. Add 500 ml brandy to each bottle. Seal and shake well. Wait two to three months and the drink will be perfect.

Hot Cocoa

As early as the seventeenth century, the province of Zeeland was famous for its chocolate cookies, made with extra bitter chocolate. In the early nineteenth century, the province boasted about fifteen chocolate factories – like De Ruijter in Vlissingen, still famous for its chocolate sprinkles. When people drank chocolate milk, they would eat cinnamon biscuits which they would dip in the hot cocoa. Apart from chocolate milk, the people in Zeeland also drank *waotersukelaode:* water (instead of milk) with chocolate. To thicken this drink, cinnamon, potato flour or an egg yolk would be added.

Preparation

Break the chocolate into pieces into a bowl and add the soft sugar and water. Place this bowl over a saucepan with hot water and melt the chocolate until smooth and thick.
In another saucepan, bring the milk to the boil. Add a little of this hot milk to the melted chocolate and stir well. Next, pour the chocolate mixture into the hot milk and leave to simmer for about 10 minutes, while stirring constantly. Serve the hot cocoa with cinnamon biscuits.

Ingredients
125 g dark chocolate
4 tbsp soft light brown sugar
3 tbsp water
1 litre milk

Porridge of Dutch Rusks

Ingredients

serves 4:

8 Dutch rusks or 'beschuiten'
20 g aniseed
1 litre milk
4 tbsp soft light brown sugar
2 tsp cinnamon
40 g butter

Preparation

Place 8 rusks in 4 deep plates and sprinkle with aniseed.
Bring the milk to the boil in a small saucepan and pour over the rusks.
Sprinkle each plate with 1 tablespoon sugar and ½ teaspoon cinnamon, and add 10 g butter.

Zaanse Schans, Noord-Holland

Semolina Porridge with Raisins

Preparation

Wash the raisins. Bring the milk with the raisins to the boil in a small saucepan and leave to simmer for about 10 minutes. Mix the semolina and the salt and add to the hot milk while stirring.

Keep stirring and slowly bring to the boil again. Continue to stir until the porridge is ready (after about 7 minutes). Serve with a lump of butter.

Ingredients

125 ml milk
80 g semolina
60 g sugar
salt
100 g raisins
butter

Thick Yogurt
'Hang-it'

Ingredients
3 litre buttermilk
soft light brown sugar
cinnamon

Preparation

Soak a clean tea towel and wring out. Place it in a colander and place the colander on top of a bowl or pan. Pour the buttermilk into the colander and leave to drain for 24 hours in a cool environment, until the buttermilk is very thick. Stir every couple of hours. Before serving, add sugar and cinnamon and serve with a Dutch rusk or *beschuit*.

In the olden days, farmers would make *hangop* ('hang-it') by hanging the tea towel with the buttermilk from a beam.

Vrijthof in Maastricht, Limburg

Rice Pudding

Preparation

Wash and rinse the rice and leave to drain thoroughly.
Pour the milk into a saucepan, add a pinch of salt and bring
to the boil.
Add the rice, bring to the boil while stirring, and leave to
simmer for 1 hour over a low heat until the rice is cooked.
Serve the rice pudding hot and sprinkle with a mixture of
sugar and cinnamon.

Ingredients
150 g rice
1 litre milk
pinch of salt
sugar
cinnamon

Crunchy Cookies with Chocolate 'Goat's feet'

Ingredients

7 egg whites
300 g sugar
450 g blanched almonds, ground
zest of 1 lemon
1 tsp cinnamon
3 packets of vanilla sugar
white edible wafer paper
75 g pure chocolate

Preparation

Preheat the oven to 160 °C. Whisk the egg whites until they form firm peaks. Add the other ingredients one by one (except for the chocolate) and mix well. Grease a baking tray and line with the wafer paper. Fill a piping bag with a wide nozzle with the egg whites and pipe onto the wafer paper. Leave to set in the fridge.

Place the baking tray in the middle of the oven and bake for 15-20 minutes. Note: the cookies should not turn brown! Leave to cool on a wire rack.

Slowly melt the chocolate while stirring. Spread a little chocolate onto the bottoms of two cookies and stick together. Dip both ends of the double cookie into the chocolate and leave to set. Repeat with the remaining cookies and chocolate. Keep the cookies in an air tight container.

Chocolate Covered Choux Buns

Preparation

In a saucepan with a thick bottom and bring the water, butter and salt to the boil.

Sieve the flour and stir into the boiling water. Continue to stir until the choux mixture forms a ball.

Remove the pan from the heat and stir the eggs into the choux mixture. Keep stirring until the mixture is glossy. Divide the mixture into 8 balls and place these onto a greased baking tray. Bake the choux buns in a preheated oven (225 °C) for 20 minutes until golden brown and doubled in size. Turn off the oven and leave the buns in the oven for another 10 minutes.

Remove the buns from the oven and with a sharp knife make a small cut in the bottom. Whip the cream, sugar and egg white together until the mixture forms stiff peaks. Fill the buns with the whipping cream.

Sieve the icing sugar and cocoa powder over a small bowl and gradually add a little whisked egg white until the mixture is thick and glossy. Cover the choux buns with the chocolate icing and leave to set.

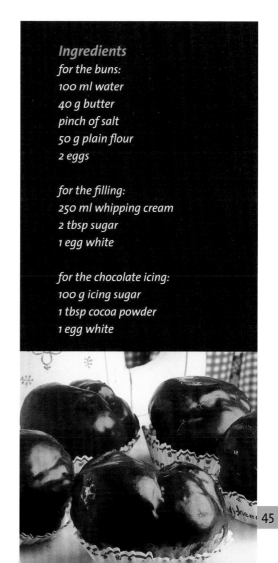

Ingredients

for the buns:
100 ml water
40 g butter
pinch of salt
50 g plain flour
2 eggs

for the filling:
250 ml whipping cream
2 tbsp sugar
1 egg white

for the chocolate icing:
100 g icing sugar
1 tbsp cocoa powder
1 egg white

45

Ingredients
3 eggs
pinch of salt
½ vanilla pod or 1 packet of vanilla sugar
125 g sugar
225 g self-raising flour
25 g cornflour

Sittard, Limburg

Eggy Cakes

Preparation

Break the eggs into a bowl and add the salt, the vanilla seeds or vanilla sugar, and the regular sugar. Whisk until you have a light, frothy mixture. Fold the flour and cornflour into the egg mixture. Stir until the mixture is smooth and leave to rest for 30 minutes.

Grease a baking tray. For each cake, drop 2 tablespoons of the mixture onto the tray; leave at least 6 cm between the cakes. Bake the eggy cakes in a preheated oven (200 °C) for 20 minutes until golden brown. Eggy cakes are enjoyed for breakfast, with a cup of coffee or tea, or as part of a cold lunch.

In the province of Noord-Brabant people will cover their eggy cake with a thick layer of butter and sugar.

Groningen Cake
with Candied Peel

Preparation

Preheat the oven to 140 °C.

Mix the flour, soft sugar, mixed spice, salt, nutmeg, cinnamon, cloves and treacle. Add the milk and stir until the mixture is smooth. Grease a cake tin with butter. Spread out half of the candied peel over the bottom of the tin. Add the cake mixture and sprinkle the remaining candied peel on top. Bake the cake for 1 hour. Leave to cool and serve.

Ingredients

250 g self-raising flour
175 g soft light brown sugar
3 tbsp treacle
pinch of salt
1 tsp cinnamon
½ tsp ground cloves
½ tsp ground nutmeg
1 tsp mixed spice
150 ml milk
150 g candied peel

Cherry Pie

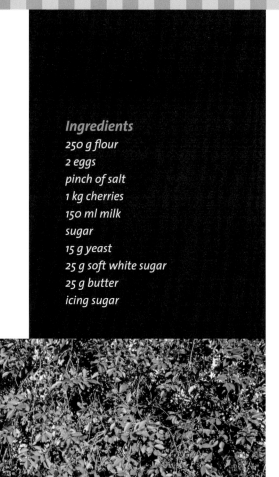

Ingredients
250 g flour
2 eggs
pinch of salt
1 kg cherries
150 ml milk
sugar
15 g yeast
25 g soft white sugar
25 g butter
icing sugar

Preparation
Sieve the flour and salt into a mixing bowl. Heat the milk until lukewarm and dissolve the yeast in a little bit of this milk. Make a well in the flour and pour in the yeast.
Add the sugar and the cubed butter plus 1 egg. Knead and gradually add the remaining lukewarm milk until the dough is soft and smooth. Cover with a moist tea towel and leave to rise for 1 hour at room temperature. Lightly flour the work surface and knead briefly. Roll out three quarters of the dough into a circle that is slightly larger than the pie tin. Grease the tin and cover the bottom and sides with the dough. Leave to rise for another 30 minutes.
Wash and stone the cherries. Prick the pie base with a fork. Divide the cherries over the base and sprinkle with 25 g soft sugar.
Roll out the rest of the dough and cut into 1½ cm wide strips. Place the strips on top of the pie, creating a nice lattice and trim the edges. Beat the remaining egg and brush over the top of the pie.
Bake on the middle shelf of the preheated oven (200 °C) for 25 minutes until golden brown.
Dust with icing sugar and leave to cool in the tin for at least 1 hour.

Almond Cookies
'Chatterboxes'

Preparation

Preheat the oven to 175 °C.

Whisk the butter until creamy and add the brown sugar.
Next, add flour, a pinch of salt and the chopped almonds.
Knead until the dough is soft and smooth. If it is too dry,
add some water.

Grease a baking tray and first bake a few cookies to test the
dough. Use 2 teaspoons and drop small heaps of dough
onto the baking tray, leaving plenty of space in between.
After 6-8 minutes, check whether the cookies have spread
enough and are nice and brown; remove the tray from the
oven. If the cookies did not spread enough, add some more
water to the dough. Now bake the cookies.

Remove the tray from the oven and leave the cookies to set.
Lift the cookies from the tray using a pallet knife and leave
them to cool. Store the cookies in an airtight container to
keep them crisp.

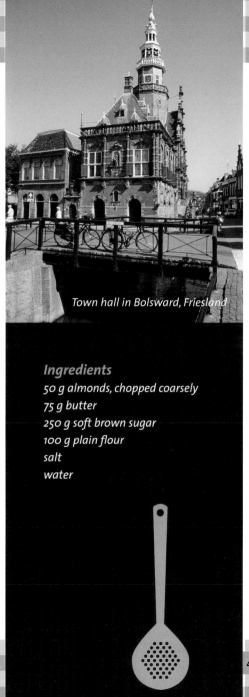

Town hall in Bolsward, Friesland

Ingredients
50 g almonds, chopped coarsely
75 g butter
250 g soft brown sugar
100 g plain flour
salt
water

New Year's Wafers

Ingredients
500 g plain flour
½ tsp salt
400 g soft white sugar
2 packets of vanilla sugar
3 eggs
250 g butter

Preparation
Sieve the flour, salt, soft sugar and the vanilla sugar. Add the eggs and the cubed butter. Knead until the dough is soft and smooth. Leave for 1½ hours and then make small balls the size of a walnut.

Heat a round waffle iron and grease. Place a dough ball in the middle and squeeze tight. Remove any dough that seeps out from the sides. Depending on your waffle iron, bake the wafers about 1½ minute until golden brown. Remove the wafer from the iron. Leave to cool on a flat surface.

Gingerbread Cake

Preparation

Preheat the oven to 150 °C.
Grease a cake tin with butter and dust with a little flour.
Mix all the ingredients into a thin and smooth batter.
Pour the batter into the cake tin and bake the cake for about 60 minutes.
To see whether the cake is done, stick a skewer into the thickest part of the cake; if the skewer comes out clean, the cake is ready.
Gingerbread cake is very nice with a cup of hot coffee.

Ingredients

500 g plain flour
500 g soft brown sugar
½ litre water
1 packet of baking powder
2 tbsp mixed spice
2 tbsp treacle
50 g butter
1 egg

Brandaris on the northern island of Terschelling

Grandma's Apple Tart

Ingredients

150 g raisins
250 g plain flour
salt
100 g sugar
150 g cold
750 g firm apples
1 tbsp lemon juice
2 tsp cinnamon
2 tbsp apricot jam
icing sugar

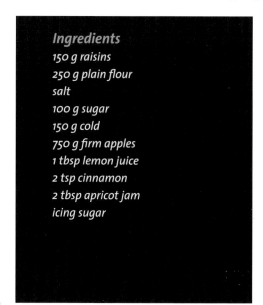

Preparation

Soak the raisins, drain and pat dry. Sieve the flour over a large bowl and add a pinch of salt and 75 g sugar. Cut the butter through the flour, using two knives. Add 2 tbsp ice water and knead with cold hands until the dough is smooth. Shape into a ball, wrap in clingfilm and place in the fridge for 1 hour.

In the meantime, peel and quarter the apples, remove the core and cut the apples into small pieces. Mix the apples in a bowl with the lemon juice, raisins, cinnamon and remaining sugar. Cover and store in the fridge.

Preheat the oven to 175 °C and grease a springform pan (diameter 24 cm). Dust the work surface and a rolling pin with flour and roll out three quarters of the dough to a circle that fits the tin, covering the bottom and sides (3 cm high). Fill the base with the apples and raisins.

Roll out the remaining dough and cut into strips. Place the strips on top of the pie, crisscrossing them to create a nice lattice.

Bake the apple tart on the middle shelf for 75 minutes until golden brown.

In the meantime, heat the jam in a small saucepan on a low heat, stirring constantly until thin and liquid. Brush the apple tart with the hot jam and leave to cool on a wire rack.

After 10 minutes remove the sides of the tin and leave to cool completely.

Dust with icing sugar.

Rice Cookies

Leftover rice pudding can be used to make rice cookies. But these cookies are so good, that you might want to make some extra anyway when cooking rice pudding.

Preparation

Beat the egg yolks in a large bowl until they are nice and light. Add the rice pudding and mix well.
Sieve the flour, cinnamon and nutmeg over the rice pudding and mix well. Beat the egg whites until they form firm peaks and fold them into the rice mixture. Melt a little butter in a frying pan. Add spoonfuls of the rice mixture and fry over a low heat until the base is golden brown and the top is dry. Flip the cookies and fry the other side until golden brown. Repeat with the remaining mixture.
Keep the fried cookies warm and serve with a little extra sugar and cinnamon.

Ingredients
2 eggs, separated
50 g sugar
500 ml rice pudding
50 g plain flour
½ tsp cinnamon
¼ tsp nutmeg

Martini tower, Groningen

Ingredients

80 g soft white sugar
200 g plain flour
½ tsp baking powder
1 egg white
180 g butter
1 packet of vanilla sugar or
    lemon zest

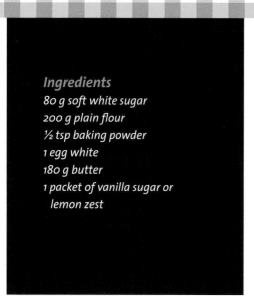

Dutch Shortbread
Sprits

Preparation

Preheat the oven to 170 °C.
Sieve the white sugar, flour and the baking powder over a large mixing bowl. In a second bowl, mix the butter, vanilla sugar or lemon zest until creamy. Add the flour and mix well. Mix in the egg white. Continue to mix until the batter is smooth and soft. Fill a piping bag with a 1 cm nozzle.
Grease a baking tray and line with greaseproof paper.
Pipe straight or wavy lines of about 4 cm; leaving at least 2 cm in between the cookies.
Place the tray in the fridge so that the batter can set.
Bake in the oven for 20-25 minutes until the shortbread is golden brown. Leave to cool on a wire rack.

Traditional Holidays & Food and Beverages

The typically Dutch *gezelligheid* requires specific food and drinks for different occasions. These tasty delights are enjoyed throughout the Netherlands and are not typical of a province or region. Easter bread and the colourful Easter eggs for example are made and eaten everywhere. Mulled wine called 'bishop's wine', gingernut cookies (*pepernoten*), fondant (*borstplaat*), marzipan, gingerbread, spice cookies (*speculaas*), and chocolate letters are abundant during the *Sinterklaas* (Saint Nicholas or Santa Clause) celebrations. And on New Year's Eve, the Dutch eat *oliebollen* (oily balls) and *appelflappen* (apple fritters).

When a baby is born, the Dutch serve rusks with aniseed sprinkles: blue and white for a boy, pink and white for a girl. And they may enjoy a glass of *kandeel*: an alcoholic drink of wine or brandy and eggs.

When a woman turns fifty, she may get a *Sara*, while a man may receive an *Abraham*. On these next pages you will find some recipes and a lot of interesting information on these specific holiday dishes and beverages.

Enjoy!

Rusks with Aniseed Sprinkles
Rusks with 'little mice'

The birth of a new baby is still celebrated with rusks with sugary aniseed sprinkles.

In the olden days, rusks or biscuits (*beschuit*) were a luxury, only to be eaten on very special days. When a baby was born and the mother and her child had survived the ordeal, that was a good enough reason to celebrate. The birth of a boy was marked with white sprinkles and the birth of a girl with pink sprinkles. Today, you can still buy aniseed sprinkles in different colours, although slightly different: blue and white for a boy, and pink and white for a girl.

The tradition of having *beschuit met muisjes* ('little mice') has superstitious origins: mice were a fertility symbol, and by having this treat, evil spirits would stay away.

Creamy Spiced Wine
Kandeel

Kandeel was traditionally served after a birth. Family and friends would be treated to this alcoholic beverage. The father would wear a satin hat with lace and a flowery dressing gown to lure evil spirits away from the mother and baby.
The cinnamon stick the father used to stir the drink would give him strength to resist the bad spirits himself. For a boy, the father would use a long cinnamon stick with bows, for a girl a shorter stick with just one bow.

Preparation
Simmer 200 ml water in a saucepan for 1 hour with ½ cinnamon stick, the cloves and lemon zest; do not let the water boil. Strain the liquid and cool.
Beat the egg yolks and the light brown sugar until the mixture is light and frothy. Stir in the cooled spiced liquid and reheat in a double boiler. Mix in the wine while stirring with the cinnamon stick.
The *kandeel* can be enjoyed warm or cold. Serve this birth beverage in a special *kandeel* glass or a porcelain bowl.

Ingredients
½ cinnamon stick
10 g cloves
zest of 1 lemon
200 ml water
6 egg yolks
100 g soft light brown sugar
1 litre Rhine wine
cinnamon stick

57

Easter

Easter (*Pasen* in the Netherlands) is a holiday with many traditions that are still honoured today. Decorating Easter eggs – originally a heathen tradition – is one of them. You can do this in the old-fashioned way, which is also environmentally-friendly! Boil the eggs in water with beetroot and they will turn red. In water with red cabbage they will become purple, green in water with spinach and yellow in water with onion peel.

But let's concentrate on the Dutch Easter bread. Making bread dough was an extremely tiring affair, as the dough had to be kneaded by hand until it was very elastic and smooth – don't forget that a modern baker can use a food processor or a hand mixer with dough hooks.

For a tasty and successful Easter bread, you need a starter – a mixture of yeast, dissolved in lukewarm milk, and a bit of flour. This starter has to rise properly (until it has doubled in size) before the dough can be made. For the following recipe, you need a cake tin of about 25 x 8½ x 8½ cm.

Easter Bread

Preparation

First, make the starter.

Next, sieve the flour over a large mixing bowl and make a well in the flour. Melt the butter. Add the lukewarm milk, the cooled melted butter, the brown sugar, salt, cinnamon, egg and the starter, and knead well until the dough is elastic and smooth. Cover with a moist tea towel and leave to rise for 1 hour at room temperature.

Rinse the sultanas, raisins and currants. Drain and dust with flour. Chop the orange peel and the candied peel and zest the lemon. Mix sultanas, raisins, currants, orange peel, candied peel, lemon zest and almonds and then add to the dough. Knead to mix well.

Roll out the dough to a circle with a diameter of 25 cm.

Roll up and place in a greased tin with the seam downwards. If you want to, you can add a roll of almond filling (see Christmas Wreath for the recipe) before rolling up the pastry again.

Leave to rise for about 30 minutes at room temperature. Place the tin on the bottom shelf in the preheated oven (225 °C) and bake the bread for 50 minutes. Dust with icing sugar, leave to cool and dust again before serving.

Ingredients
500 g plain flour
40 g yeast
300 ml milk
100 g butter
75 g soft light brown sugar
½ tsp salt
1 tsp cinnamon
1 egg
125 g sultanas
125 g raisins
250 g currants
25 g candied orange peel
25 g candied peel
zest of 1 lemon
25 g sliced almonds
icing sugar

Mulled Wine
'Bishop's wine'

Ingredients
for 8 glasses:
1 orange
1 lemon
20 cloves
1 bottle of red wine, like Bordeaux
100 ml water
¼ cinnamon stick
2 tbsp sugar

Tip

Do not serve this hot wine in your best glasses, as the heat may break them. Tea or coffee glasses or mugs are best.

Preparation

Brush and clean the orange and the lemon and stick 10 cloves in each piece of fruit. Add the orange and lemon, the wine, water, cinnamon and sugar to a saucepan (not aluminium). Cover and bring almost to the boil over a low heat. Note: the wine should not boil. Place the pan on a burner and leave to simmer for 1½ hours over the lowest possible heat.
Use a slotted spoon to remove the orange, lemon and cinnamon stick from the pan. Turn up the heat and bring the wine almost to the boil. Pour the wine into 8 glasses and serve hot.

Fondant

Preparation

Prepare the moulds for the fondant: dust with flour and place on a wet piece of greaseproof paper, or moisten with water and place on a greased baking tray.

Mix in a small saucepan sugar, milk and cocoa powder. Heat and simmer over a low heat until the mixture has thickened and reached the soft ball stage. Continue to stir. Never heat the sugar mixture for more than 10 minutes.

Remove the pan from the heat and leave to cool while stirring until you are ready to pour the cream into the moulds. Fill the moulds and leave to set. Remove the moulds, but be very careful as the fondant can easily break.

You can replace the milk by whipping cream (not whipped). Instead of cocoa powder you can use vanilla extract (to make vanilla fondant) or 2½ tbsp strong coffee (mocha fondant).

Ingredients
for chocolate fondant:
500 g sugar
125 ml milk
2½ tbsp cocoa powder

61

Ingredients
200 g self-raising flour
100 g butter
125 g soft light brown sugar
pinch of salt
2 tbsp milk
15 g mixed spice
20 blanched almonds, halved

Speculaas Pieces

Preparation
Mix the self-raising flour and the cubed butter in a large mixing bowl. Add the brown sugar, some salt, the milk and the mixed spice. Knead with cold hands until the pastry is smooth. Cover and leave overnight.
Roll out the pastry onto a greased baking tray; the pastry should be about 1 cm thick. Decorate with halved almonds. Place the tray in the bottom half of the preheated oven (150 °C) and bake the *speculaas* for 45 minutes until nice and brown. Remove from the oven and leave to cool on the baking tray. Break the *speculaas* into uneven bits.

Speculaas is a typically Dutch treat and is usually served in the winter months. Small cookies and larger dolls are also made using special wooden moulds.

Christmas Wreath

Preparation

Grind the almonds. Mix the ground almonds, sugar, egg, lemon zest and juice and 2 tablespoons water in a mixing bowl; mix well. Grind this mixture twice so that there are absolutely no more lumps. Make this almond filling several days before, preferably even weeks before baking. Covered with foil and store in an airtight jar.

Roll out the puff pastry to a strip of 70 cm x 10 cm. Knead the black cherries into the almond filling and form a sausage of about 60 cm. Place the filling in the middle of the pastry. Moisten the long edge of the pastry strip and fold over the filling; press down carefully. Shape the long 'sausage' into an O and place on a moist baking tray; make sure the seam points downwards.

Beat the egg and brush onto the pastry. Place the pastry on the middle shelf of the preheated oven (200 °C) bake for 40 minutes until golden brown.

Mix the icing sugar and a few drops of water and glaze the wreath. Garnish with glacé cherries and candied orange peel.

Ingredients

for the almond filling (400 g):
175 g blanched almonds
175 g sugar
1 egg
zest of ½ lemon
1½ tsp lemon juice
2 tbsp water

for the bake:
300 g puff pastry, defrosted if
   necessary
400 g almond filling
10 black cherries, halved
1 egg
50 g icing sugar
water
glacé cherries
candied orange peel

Apple Fritters

Ingredients

for about 25:
6 large firm apples
pinch of salt
1 egg
150 g self-raising flour
225 ml milk
3 litre vegetable oil
icing sugar
cinnamon

Preparation

Peel the apples and carefully cut out the core with a corer. Cut the apples into 1 cm thick slices.

Take a bowl and add the flour. Make a well and add the egg and salt. Gradually pour in the milk while stirring, to make a nice and smooth batter. Stir in ½ tablespoon vegetable oil. Heat the oil in a deep frying pan. Dip the slices of apples in the batter, shake of any excess and fry in the hot oil until they are golden brown and crisp.

Remove the fritters from the oil using a slotted spoon and leave to drain on kitchen paper. Sprinkle with icing sugar and cinnamon if you like.

Oily Balls
'Oliebollen'

Preparation

Sieve the flour in a large mixing bowl and make a well. In a separate bowl, dissolve the yeast in a little lukewarm milk and add to the well in the flour. Gradually add the remaining milk and some salt. Continue to stir until the batter is nice and smooth.

Rinse the sultanas, raisins and currants and leave to drain thoroughly. Peel the apples and remove the core. Chop the apples and candied peel. Add the sultanas, raisins, currants, apples and candied peel to the batter and mix well. Cover the batter and leave to rise for 1 hour at room temperature.

Heat the oil in a deep-frying pan to 190 °C and place plenty of kitchen paper on the work surface. Use two tablespoons or an ice scoop to shape the balls and carefully drop them into the hot oil.

Fry the *oliebollen* (5 at the time) for 5 minutes until golden brown. After about 3 minutes, the ball will turn over automatically; if they don't, you turn them.

Remove the *oliebollen* from the oil using a slotted spoon and leave to drain on the kitchen paper.

Dust with icing sugar before serving.

Ingredients

for about 25:
500 g plain flour
500 ml milk, lukewarm
40 g yeast
pinch of salt
75 g sultanas
75 g raisins
75 g currants
50 g candied peel
2 firm apples
3 litre vegetable oil

Ingredients

Ingredients
600 g plain flour
salt
1 tbsp baking powder
300 g soft light brown sugar
350 g butter
50 ml milk
3 tbsp mixed spice
almonds
icing sugar
water
cotton wool

Sara and Abraham

In the Bible (John 8:57) it says: 'You are not yet fifty years old… and you have seen Abraham!' The Dutch decided it would be a good idea to celebrate a man's (or a woman's) fiftieth birthday by presenting them with a baked Abraham (or Sara). In some regions of the Netherlands, these figures consist of large pieces of meat – you also see huge inflatable Abrahams placed in the front yard of the birthday boy.

The cake that was originally used for the Abraham doll was more like bread, but later gingerbread (see recipe) or bread with an almond filling was also used.

Preparation

Sieve the flour, salt, baking powder and the brown sugar over a bowl. Gradually add the cubed butter, the milk and the mixed spice and knead with cool hands until the pastry is nice and smooth. Leave the pastry in a cool place overnight. Roll out the pastry to a rectangle of about 50 cm long and 1 cm thick. Cut out a human figure of 50 cm and decorate with almonds and score lines (with the back of knife) to make an Abraham or a Sara.

Place the figure on a greased baking tray and bake in a preheated oven (200 °C) for 35 minutes until golden brown. Leave to cool.

Mix some icing sugar with a few drops of water to make icing. Stick a cotton wool beard onto Abraham using the icing.

Old-Fashioned Liqueurs

Bitterkoekjeslikeur
Macaroon liqueur

A liqueur made from almonds and peach stones, meant for 12½, 25 and 50 years wedding anniversaries. To wash away any possible bitter memories (macaroons are called 'bitter cookies' in Dutch).

Bruidstranen
'Tears of the bride'

Gold and silver leaf in a liqueur with a heavenly aroma. The liqueur was served at weddings. Clever wives would give their husband a glass of this liqueur every time the husband did something bad – to remind him of his wedding vows.

Eau de ma tante

A drink with Dutch cherries and Belgian sour cherries in brandy, fresh peaches in eau de vie, and the juice of fresh raspberries, mixed with eau de vie de framboise and Zuger kirsch. The drink is sometimes made with oranges and bitter almonds.

Hansje in de kelder
'Little Hans in the basement'

A liqueur containing several interesting ingredients, such as apricot, orange, cinnamon, bergamot and lemon. It was originally served in a specific beaker to announce a pregnancy – an occasion to which friends and family were all invited.

Hempje licht op
'Lift up your undershirt'

When Holland was still a seafaring nation, this drink was popular among sailors, as it was used to solve bowel problems. Contains orange, liquorice, fennel, cocoa and vanilla.

Hoe langer hoe liever
'The longer the better'

Brandy containing elderberries, passion fruit, vanilla, honey and a 'secret' mixture of liquorice, coriander, lovage, Indian cloves, cinnamon and horseradish. A drink for people who are in love and want to stay together forever.

Juffertje in het groen
'Innocent little lady'

A liqueur made from e.g. citrus peel, star anise flowers, mint, orange and vanilla. The various taste combinations are created by using specific herbs. The liqueur was said to be enjoyed by elderly ladies who wanted to feel young again.

Kwartier na vijven
'Quarter past five'

Also known as 'quarter to five'. The ingredients may vary, but the drink usually contains sour oranges, fresh oranges and lemon juice, mixed with brandy. This drink was served in most bars around five o'clock – hence the name.

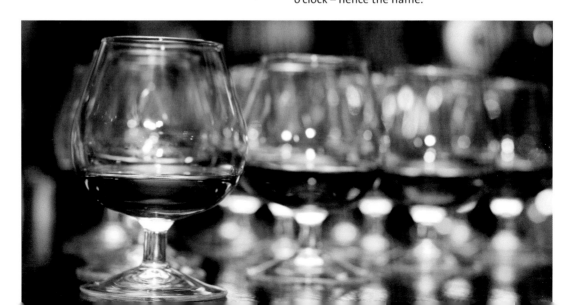

Naveltje bloot
'Naked belly button'

Made from the peel of among others things overripe oranges, Sicilian lemons, the peel of bitter oranges, lime juice, vanilla and caraway seeds. The drink was originally served at parties where the upcoming birth and the health of the mother-to-be were discussed.

Pruimpje prik in
'Plum prick in'

A lovely liqueur made from plums and reine claude, enriched with honey and vanilla. The plums were pierced to enhance the taste.

Papegaaiensoep
'Parrot soup'

An interesting liqueur with almonds, walnuts, hazelnuts, chestnuts and peanuts. With the colour of weak tea and a name that is supposed to disguise the fact that the tipplers were actually drinking alcohol.

Roosje zonder doornen
'A rose without thorns'

Making a rose liqueur is quite complicated, as the taste can easily become overwhelming. However, when distilled in exactly the right way, the four different roses combined taste wonderfully.

The Twelve Provinces
of the Netherlands

The province of **Groningen** is in the very North of the Netherlands. It boasts peace and quiet, coastlines and dykes, the second oldest university of the country, loads of students, and earthquakes – the latter due to decades of gas drilling.

Drenthe is famous for its dolmens, cycle paths and heathland. The city of Emmen has one of the best zoos in the country, and in Assen you will find the Drents Museum with wonderful exhibitions.

Friesland has many lovely old cities and numerous lakes that are ideal for all kinds of water sports. Close to the southern town of Lemmer, you find the biggest, still active steam pumping station in the world: the Ir. D.F. Woudagemaal.

The city of Zwolle in the green province of **Overijssel** has an incredible museum and the most beautiful bookshop in a church. The small town of Giethoorn is famous for its canals, boats and also the thousands of Chinese tourists that frequent it in the summer months.

▲ In **Gelderland** you find the Veluwe National Park, which you can explore by bike (free!). In the park you find the Kröller Müller Museum, 'a second home to Vincent van Gogh'.

▼ **Utrecht** is situated right in the middle of the Netherlands. Visit the old city of Utrecht with its beautiful canals, bars and restaurants. The highest point of the city is the famous Dom tower.

Limburg is the most southern bit of the Netherlands and borders Germany and Belgium. The province is famous for its *vlaaien* (pies) and carnival. The capital Maastricht has a chic and bohemian atmosphere.

Noord-Brabant is the large province in the south. The main cities here are Eindhoven (home of the football club PSV), Breda (a lovely city close to the Biesbosch National Park), Den Bosch (birth place of Jheronimus Bosch) and Tilburg (Museum De Pont).

Noord-Holland is in the northwest. The region boasts beautiful beaches, traditional towns like Volendam, Edam and Marken, and great cities such as Haarlem and Amsterdam.

Flevoland is the youngest province, since 1986. All of Flevoland used to be water: the three polders are the result of land reclamation. The former islands of Urk and Schokland are great places to visit. Don't forget your camera!

Zeeland lies south of Zuid-Holland, just north of Belgium. This very wet province is the home of most of the Delta Works, for which the Dutch are world-famous. The Delta Works – protection against the sea – were started after the great flooding of 1953.

▲ **Zuid-Holland**, along the North Sea coast, is in fact one large urban agglomeration. Here you find the cities of Rotterdam, The Hague, Delft, Leiden and Zoetermeer with several universities and many great museums.

After the bombings in the Second World War, **Rotterdam** was rebuilt and is now (partly) a very modern city. The port of Rotterdam is the largest cargo port in Europe and the tenth largest in the world.

▲ **Amsterdam** is the capital of the Netherlands and the most populous city of the country. Visit the Rijks Museum, the Van Gogh Museum, the Hermitage or the Anne Frank House. And please don't think that one day is enough!

The Hague is the seat of the Dutch government and parliament. King Willem-Alexander works in The Hague. You can also find lots of embassies and international organisations in this city, including the International Criminal Court and the International Court of Justice.

National Anthem

The Dutch national anthem is called the Wilhelmus, which became the country's national anthem in 1932. The entire anthem has no less than fifteen verses, but fortunately only the first and sometimes the sixth verse are sung at official or festive occasions. The first letters of the verses form the official name of the real Wilhelmus: Willem van Nassov.

Dutch

Wilhelmus van Nassouwe
ben ik, van Duitschen bloed,
den vaderland getrouwe
blijf ik tot in den dood.
Een Prinse van Oranje
ben ik, vrij, onverveerd,
den Koning van Hispanje
heb ik altijd geëerd.

Translation

William of Nassau,
am I of German descent.
True to the fatherland,
I'll be until death.
A prince of Orange,
am I free and brave.
The king of Spain,
I have always honoured.

79